Forew

I expected my first meeting with Dr. Zez about a half-hour. Two and half hours later when our meeting concluded, I knew I had met a very special educator.

When I met Dr. Zezula in June 1994, I asked her opinion regarding the information I had collected for my first book, *The Pet Professional's Comparative Reference Guide to Premium Dry Dog Food*. She reviewed the information and then proceeded to steer me through an educational process that continues to this day. With her patient explanation and review, my first book soon saw the light of day.

After publication, I was surprised to learn that veterinary and pet industry professionals were asking for basic pet nutrition information. I told Dr. Zezula about this feedback and the outline for *Doc Z's Canine Nutrition Primer* and *Doc Z 's Feline Nutrition Primer* was created.

As the project evolved, it became clear that basic nutrition information was not enough. The scope was extended to include a discussion (with examples) of pet food math, an annotated bibliography, a section on understanding pet food labels, and a glossary of technical terms.

Doc Z's Feline Nutrition Primer is a terrific introduction to the subject of feline nutrition. For someone looking for basics or a quick refresher, the fundamentals are here. For experienced professionals, the pet food math discussion and worksheets along with the annotated bibliography will prove to be most useful.

Howard D. Coffman, Author
The Pet Professional's Comparative Reference Guide to Premium Dry Dog Food
The Dry Dog Food Reference
The Cat Food Reference

Nashua, New Hampshire

Doc Z's Feline Nutrition Primer

By:

Jerilee A. Zezula, D.V.M.

Associate Professor of Applied Animal Science
Thompson School of Applied Science
University of New Hampshire

PigDog™ Press
Nashua, N.H. USA

Doc Z's Feline Nutrition Primer

PigDog™ Press
427-3 Amherst Street, Suite 331
Nashua, N. H. 03063-1258 USA

Disclaimer

This book is designed to provide information in regard to the subject matter covered. It is sold with the understanding that the publisher and author are not engaged in rendering professional services. If expert assistance is required, the services of a competent professional should be sought. Every effort has been made to make this book complete and as accurate as possible. However, there may be mistakes both typographical and in content. Therefore this text should be used as a general guide.

The purpose of this book is to educate. The author and publisher, and any and all persons or entities involved in any way in the preparation, publication, sale or distribution of this book disclaim all responsibility for any action taken in reliance upon any information contained in this book. You have the responsibility to check all material you read here before relying on it.

The author and publisher shall have neither liability nor responsibility to any person or entity with respect to any loss or damage caused, or alleged to be caused, directly or indirectly by the information contained in this book.

Disclaimer Used By Permission: Whatever Happened to Justice. Richard J. Maybury. Blue Stocking Press, P.O. Box 1014, Placerville, CA 95667. 1993.

Trademarks

PigDog™, PetMath™, Sleuth Cat™, and Sleuth Dog™ are trademarks of PigDog™ Press, Nashua, N.H. 03063. All other product, brand or tradenames, service marks, or registered marks are the property of their respective owners.

Special Thanks

To the authors and publishers who contributed copies of their books for review and deposit into the Applied Animal Science Library at the Thompson School of Applied Science, University of New Hampshire.

Contents

Doc Z's
Feline
Nutrition
Primer

Feline Nutrition: A Primer

Introduction

The cat, our #1 household pet, is a true carnivore. The cat's teeth, digestive system, and internal biochemistry are designed for taking full advantage of animal flesh as the major food source.

As with all mammals, the cat needs proteins, fats, carbohydrates, vitamins, minerals, and water. The proteins, fats, and carbohydrates provide energy and contribute to growth and tissue synthesis. The vitamins, minerals, and water participate in the chemical reactions of the body and are incorporated into living tissues.

If we look at the wild cousins of the domestic cat, we see a predator who kills and eats her prey. Unlike the dog, the cat does not usually eat the whole animal. She will eat the flesh, but avoid the guts and other "distasteful" tissue. Wild cats are not usually seen eating berries, vegetables, and greens as a wild dog might. There is good reason for this. The cat's digestive system cannot effectively breakdown this material. It would only serve as roughage and go through

undigested! Even partially digested stomach contents of herbivorous prey cannot be effectively digested and metabolized by cats.

Domestic cats share our homes and few exclusively rely on hunting to provide their food. While the house cat still possesses the prey instinct, she depends on her owner to provide the proper diet to meet her needs.

Cat owners must realize that cats are still true carnivores. Even with domestication, the cat's anatomy and physiology have not changed; she is still built like her wild cousins.

Required Nutrients

Protein

A good cat food should contain digestible animal-source proteins that provide the essential amino acids in adequate amounts.

Feline Nutrition: A Primer

Proteins are organic chemical compounds and a major component of all living organisms. Proteins are made up of small sub-units known as amino acids. Amino acids arranged in specific amounts and patterns form many different types of complex proteins.

Living organisms put together the proteins that make up their structure by combining amino acids through complex biochemical mechanisms. These proteins build and repair body structures, form enzymes, hormones, and body fluids, or provide energy. Cats need eleven specific amino acids to make the proteins they use and they *must* come from the protein they eat. These are "essential amino acids."

If a cat has these eleven amino acids in her diet in adequate amounts, her internal biochemistry can make the others as needed. A cat is biologically an animal. The proteins that make up her body are similar to those of other animals. These proteins usually contain most of the essential amino acids cats need because they often use the same "building blocks."

Plants, as grain, seed, or bean, also contain protein and therefore, amino acids. The "essential" amino acids found in plants do not come as close to matching all the needs of the cat as does animal protein. Some plant material has a "protective carbohydrate coating." These chemical bonds cannot be digested by cats and the protein and amino acid present in some plant material cannot be digested and absorbed.

Please note that there is not one "magic" protein source that contains all the essential amino acids in adequate amounts. The food provided should contain primarily *animal sources* of digestible proteins. Also, some highly digestible plant sources can provide some essential amino acids and other required nutrients.

The total amount of protein required by cats is very high compared to dogs. The cat, being a true obligate carnivore, has a digestive system and metabolism that "prefers" protein for an energy source. A higher percentage of protein must be in the cat's diet to meet these needs.

Feline Nutrition: A Primer

Essential Amino Acids

Arginine
Histidine
Isoleucine
Leucine
Lysine
Methionine
Phenylalanine
Tryptophane
Threonine
Valine

Taurine (unique to cats)

Carbohydrates

Carbohydrates provide some energy and give bulk.

Carbohydrates are organic compounds made of carbon, hydrogen, and oxygen molecules arranged in compounds ranging from simple to complex. The most simple molecules are often called sugars. The more complex molecules are called starch, cellulose, and lignin. Plant material is made up of a high percentage of carbohydrates and serves primarily as a carbohydrate source.

Animal source carbohydrates can be found in muscle and liver tissues. Carbohydrates when eaten can serve as an energy source - if they can be digested. Please note that the feline digestive system is not able to digest many complex carbohydrates and they will pass unscathed through the digestive tract. This type of carbohydrate serves as roughage or provides bulk which aides digestion. Cats are carnivores and do not need carbohydrates for energy if there is adequate protein and fat their diet.

Fat

Fats provide concentrated energy, essential fatty acids, and a source of fat-soluble vitamins.

Fats, too, are complex molecules broken down by the digestive system into smaller molecules called fatty acids. Fatty acids are used as an efficient source of fuel for energy, and as a "building block" in making hormones, skin and coat oils, membranes, and as parts of body cells.

Feline Nutrition: A Primer

Specific fatty acids must be in the diet and these are called "essential fatty acids." Of these, arachidonic acid is found only in animal source fats. This again emphasizes the carnivorous nature of the cat.

As fats are digested, certain dissolved vitamins become nutritionally available. Fat sources can be both plant and animal in origin. Some essential fatty acids are more available in one source than in another. Vitamin A must be obtained from animal source fat as cats cannot convert plant origin beta carotene into Vitamin A as omnivores and dogs can. Fat is also a major contributor to the palatability of a food. The odors from fats will really attract a cat!

Essential Fatty Acids

Linoleic Acid
Linolenic Acid*
Arachidonic Acid (animal source)
Eicosapentaenoic Acid
   (animal source)*
Docosahexaenoic Acid
   (animal source)*

* If adequate linoleic and arachidonic acid are present, the three others may not be needed in the diet. However, cats seem to thrive when they are in the diet.

Vitamins

Vitamins must be present in the cat's diet to insure proper metabolism.

Vitamins are tiny organic compounds necessary for the complicated biochemical reactions all animals need to function. Vitamins are found in both plant and animal material. Cats can actually manufacture some of the vitamins they need, so their diet only has to provide what they cannot make. Vitamins are often part of the plant or animal material that makes up cat food. Sometimes they are manufactured independently and added to the food.

Vitamins are classified as water soluble or fat soluble. Fat soluble vitamins are usually an integral part of the animal source fat.

Feline Nutrition: A Primer

Water soluble vitamins are often added specifically to the diet. The wild cat acquires vitamins from the digestion of prey which contain the vitamins.

Water Soluble Vitamins

B Complex Vitamins
(Thiamine, Riboflavin,
Pantothenic Acid,
Pyridoxine, Biotin,
Folic Acid, Niacin,
Cobalamin, Choline)
Vitamin C*

Fat Soluble Vitamins

Vitamin A**
(only from animal sources)
Vitamin D*
Vitamin E
Vitamin K*

*Can be synthesized or made by the cat either from precursors or intestinal microbes.

** See comment under **Fat**

Minerals

Minerals have many functions ranging from bone formation to catalyst for biochemical reactions.

Minerals are inorganic elements necessary for growth, reproduction, and proper function. Required minerals are often grouped into macrominerals (required in relatively large amounts), and microminerals (required in trace amounts).

Because minerals are inorganic (not made or necessarily part of living things), they can be obtained directly from the environment or second hand from eating food that has minerals within its ingredients; e.g. calcium in bone meal and iron in meat. The wild cat gets minerals from eating the whole prey - bones, ground-in dirt, muscles, eggs, egg shells, etc. Another mineral source is drinking water from ponds or streams. The exact requirements of each mineral in a cat's diet has not been accurately determined.

Feline Nutrition: A Primer

Required Minerals and Their Functions

Mineral	Function
Calcium	Bone formation, nerve transmission, muscle contraction, enzymes, and cardiac function
Phosphorus	Same as calcium
Magnesium	Bone formation, biochemical reactions, protein synthesis. Extra amounts of this mineral also pose a problem for cats because of magnesium's involvement in feline urological syndrome (see glossary)
Sulfur	Amino acid, protein, and hormone formation
Iron	Hemoglobin, myoglobin, all body cells, and biochemical reactions
Copper	Same as iron, also liver function
Zinc	Biochemical reactions
Manganese	Biochemical reactions
Iodine	Thyroid hormone production
Selenium	Works with Vitamin E, and biochemical reactions

Feline Nutrition: A Primer

Water

Water is the most important nutrient. If not present in adequate amounts the cat can die.

The importance of water cannot be overemphasized. The cells of a cat's body contain 80% water and most biochemical reactions require water. Some water may be contained in the food sources, but fresh clean drinking water should always be available.

Energy

Everything a cat does requires energy - breathing, running, growing, eating, reproducing, nursing kittens, maintaining body temperature, napping . . . This energy is produced by complex biochemical reactions that require fuel in the form of sugars, fatty acids, or amino acids. These are the components of proteins, carbohydrates, and fats. Therefore proteins, carbohydrates, and fats are the sources of energy in the diet.

Because of the chemical nature of these compounds, equal amounts of carbohydrates and proteins provide roughly the same amount of energy. An equal amount of fat will produce twice as much energy. Fat is called "concentrated" energy.

The wild cat hunts when she sees prey and when she is hungry. Hunger is triggered when her body senses a need for energy. If she kills when she is not hungry, she hides the food until she needs it. She does not consciously balance her diet. Her diet "balances" only if she eats the right variety of food.

The domestic cat should be fed to meet her energy requirements. If a cat takes in more energy than she needs, she stores the excess as fat. If she does not take in enough energy, she uses her body fat and glycogen (stored carbohydrate) for energy first. When these are gone, she will then begin to use the proteins that make up her muscle tissues.

Feline Nutrition: A Primer

The "Best" Diet

Pet owners should choose the best diet for their cats. How does one choose from the myriad of foods available from the grocery store, pet store, feed store, and veterinary clinic? Some tips:

Know the age and life-style requirements of your cat

Growing kittens have different requirements than adult cats. Active cats have different requirements from sedentary cats. Cat food feeding guidelines are based on estimated energy needs of cats fed in research conditions. An owner should modify the guidelines to suit their cat's life-style.

Know how to read pet food labels

Much information can be obtained from the pet food label. It is the first screening device in selecting a good food. Owners should pay attention to the "Nutritional Adequacy" statement and look for "feeding studies" in the statement. This means that the food has been successfully fed to cats in that life-stage category.

The ingredient list is also important. Items are listed from highest to lowest amounts. Is the ingredient listed more than once in different forms? The *sources* of protein are very important to note. Where is the meat-based protein on the list?

The "Guaranteed Analysis Statement" needs to be reviewed but only after converting the percentages to dry matter values. (See Worksheet on page 47.)

There are many references on how to read pet food labels available from the pet food companies and other sources. Ingredient definitions can be obtained from the *AAFCO Official Publication*. (See page 21 for ordering information.)

Consult the next section for a more complete discussion on *Understanding Pet Food Labels*.

Feline Nutrition: A Primer

Compare Prices

Many diets appear the same on the label but there is a significant difference in price. If a price is extremely low, there is often a reason for it. If a price is extremely high, an owner may be paying for a brand name or a current fad.

Try the food

Will the cat eat it? The best food in the world is no good if the cat won't eat it!

While on this diet, does the cat act healthy and vigorous? How does the cat look? How much stool and of what consistency does the cat produce? Does the cat maintain a good weight? Does it act hungry between meals? Is the hair coat smooth and glossy, and the skin moist?

Cats are individuals. The "best" food for one cat may not be the "best" for another. Remember, do not hesitate to try another food if your cat is not comfortable with the one you are feeding.

Read and Ask Questions

The knowledge base of information about cat nutrition is expanding very quickly as veterinary scientists study the #1 pet. Like dogs, there is a lot of myth surrounding the feeding of cats. Owners should read and ask questions of veterinarians and pet food companies before deciding on a little known or questionable feeding recommendation.

Understanding
Pet Food
Labels

Understanding Pet Food Labels

Disclaimer

The subject of pet food labeling is a complex regulatory issue. The following discussion is an introduction to the topic of pet food labeling and regulation and represents the author's understanding of the subject determined from basic research and limited feedback from knowledgeable persons involved with pet food regulations. *Use it as a basis for your own inquiry.*

Introduction

Each state has its own specific regulations governing what is permitted or not permitted to be printed on a pet food label. What is common however, is that all state regulations are based on guidelines developed by an organization known as AAFCO.

Before we get into the specifics of pet food labeling, let's first introduce the organization that influences and recommends pet food labeling regulations to the states.

AAFCO

AAFCO (Association of American Feed Control Officials) is an organization whose members are State, Federal, and Provincial officers "charged by law with execution of the State, Province, Dominion, and Federal laws in the Continent of North America, Hawaii, and Puerto Rico regulating the production, labeling, distribution, and sale of animal feeds and livestock remedies." (By-Laws, p. 54)

"A basic goal of AAFCO is to provide a mechanism, for developing, and implementing, uniform and equitable laws, regulations, standards, definitions and enforcement policies for regulating the manufacture, labeling, distribution and sale of animal feeds; resulting in safe, effective, and useful feeds.

The Association thereby promotes new ideas and innovative procedures and urges their adoption by member agencies, for uniformity." (By-Laws, p. 62)

Understanding Pet Food Labels

AAFCO members are state feed control officials and representatives from the U.S. Food and Drug Administration. In addition, liaisons from industry sit on the various working committees that evaluate and recommend feed and ingredient definitions, pet food label requirements, pet food nutritional profiles, and many other issues.

Please note that AAFCO committees propose and recommend policies to the membership. It is up to the membership to approve the recommendations at the August annual meeting. Once approved they are published in the annual *AAFCO Official Publication*.

Although pet food industry representatives participate in the committee research and evaluation process, they do not vote for final acceptance. At this time, there are no liaison representatives from any consumer organization. There are liaison representatives from industry publications and assoc-iations, pet food manufacturers, and pet food ingredient suppliers.

Pet Food Labeling Requirements

The following is based on the AAFCO Model Feed Law and Model Regulations described in the *1995 AAFCO Official Publication*. The Model Feed Law and Model Regulations are guidelines for the states to use as they develop their state specific regulations. It is safe to say, that the AAFCO Model Feed Law and Regulations are the most stringent set of regulations a state could adopt.

These items and other specific guidelines concerning language, print size, and product claims are found in the Model Pet Food Regulations published in the *AAFCO Official Publication*. AAFCO guidelines specify that the following items *must* appear on pet food labels.

- Brand Name
- Purpose Statement (dog or cat food)
- Guaranteed Analysis
- List of Ingredients (ordered by weight)
- Directions for Use

Understanding Pet Food Labels

- Name, Address, & Zip of Manufacturer
- Quantity Statement
- Claim that it meets AAFCO nutritional adequacy

Pet Food Ingredient Lists

Pet food ingredient lists provide a lot of information. Some things to remember are:

- Ingredients are listed in "descending order of predominance by weight"

- Ingredients may be used in different ways by different manufacturers.

For example, barley could be considered a protein source as well as a carbohydrate source.

The Food and Drug Administration (FDA) requires pet food manufacturers to list the ingredients and sub-ingredients in descending order of predominance by weight.

Sub-ingredients could be an ingredient added by a supplier or an ingredient used to carry a vitamin mixture in the product. Exceptions are documented in the Code of Federal Regulations, 21 CFR Part 501.100. In many cases, the manufacturer decision to include or exclude a sub-ingredient depends of the amount of that ingredient in the final product.

If an ingredient requires a preservative (anti-oxidant), the preservative must be listed with that ingredient. For example: Poultry Fat (Mixed Tocopherols used as a preservative).

In this case, Poultry Fat is preserved by Mixed Tocopherols. Take note that the ingredient and its preservative (found in parenthesis) are listed together, in the same phrase.

In the case where the preservative is added to the product, not the ingredient, it appears in the ingredient list as any other ingredient. For example: BHA (a preservative).

Generally speaking, a preservative is used when a fat or protein source is present. Preservatives are necessary to prevent spoilage. If the

Understanding Pet Food Labels

fat or protein source spoils or goes rancid, it could negatively affect the health of your pet. That's why it's important to purchase food that is fresh.

Sometimes an ingredient list may list several related grain ingredients in close proximity on the ingredient list. This listing technique is called "splitting."

For example, a dry pet food label contains the following as its first four ingredients: Poultry Meal, Rice Flour, Rice Bran, Ground Rice.

Remember, ingredients are listed by weight. In this case Poultry Meal is listed first. However, it is quite possible that if all the "rice ingredients" were listed as one ingredient, they would weigh more than the Poultry Meal and; therefore, rice would have to be listed before Poultry Meal. Also remember, the type of processing of an ingredient, especially grains, affects its digestibility; so, splitting does give you some valuable information.

This practice is not unique to pet foods. It applies to human foods as well. Reading any product label will give you a better understanding of its content. For everything we buy, it's important to read labels carefully. And the old adage, "Buyer Beware" has stood the test of time, and for good reason.

Ingredient Definitions

You could write a book on ingredient definitions. And in fact, AAFCO already has. In the *AAFCO Official Publication*, which is updated annually, is listed the feed term and ingredient definitions commonly used in animal feeds.

Many of the ingredient definitions also apply to human foods. These definitions are recognized by the Food and Drug Administration (FDA), and are considered the regulatory definition of a feed ingredient. Not all ingredients used in pet foods have an AAFCO definition. Some are very common like salt; others may not have gone through the rigorous and lengthy definition process.

Generally, the first few ingredients contain most of the weight of the

Understanding Pet Food Labels

product. Subsequent ingredients usually provide the vitamins and minerals needed to balance the nutritional needs of the animal. A subset of the AAFCO Ingredient Definitions can be found in *The Cat Food Reference*, available from PigDog™ Press.

Guaranteed Analysis

The Guaranteed Analysis required on pet food labels states minimum or maximum nutrient value for a particular dog or cat food.

Guaranteed Analysis values are frequently derived from "As Is" or "As Fed" values compiled by the pet food manufacturer from the averaged results of numerous laboratory analyses. Many manufacturers provide these additional analyses upon request.

For dog and cat foods, the following values are *required* in the Guaranteed Analysis section:

Crude Protein	Minimum %
Crude Fat	Minimum %
Crude Fiber	Maximum %
Moisture	Maximum %

Some manufacturers provide additional "guarantees." They are not required, but provide useful information.

The Guaranteed Analysis is how the manufacturer states on the package its regulatory requirement of minimum/maximum nutrient content.

AAFCO Required Nutritional Adequacy Statement

There are two ways AAFCO and pet food manufacturers state the nutritional adequacy of pet foods:

- pet food testing protocol completion
    "animal feeding tests"
- pet food nutritional profile compliance
    "is formulated"

In each case, the manufacturer prepares and has available on file at their company, a specific affidavit identifying the method used to comply with the nutritional adequacy requirement. This affidavit is available on request only to state feed control officials.

Understanding Pet Food Labels

Regulation PF2 allows for several different adequacy statements. Most often, statement (a) or (b) is used. Statements are product specific and in addition to being found on product packaging may also be found in company literature. It is possible that different foods offered by the same manufacturer may have different AAFCO nutritional adequacy statements.

In the case of "feeding studies," several different conditions apply:

- Growth Foods
  Puppies & kittens are fed for 10 weeks
- Gestation and Lactation Foods
  Adults are fed for 3 months
- Maintenance Foods
  Adults are fed for a minimum of 6 months

In the case of "is formulated," laboratory analysis is used to ensure the food meets the nutritional profiles described in the *AAFCO Official Publication* for growth, adult maintenance and/or all life stages.

Regulation PF2. Label Format and Labeling (excerpt p. 109)

(1)   A claim that the pet food meets the requirements of one or more of the recognized categories of nutritional adequacy: gestation, lactation, growth, maintenance, and complete for all life stages, as those categories are set forth in regulations PF2(l) and (m). The claim shall be stated as one of the following (*emphasis added*):

   (a)   (Name of product) *is formulated* to meet the nutritional levels established by the AAFCO Dog (or Cat) Food Nutrient Profiles for ____. (Blank is to be completed by using the stage of the pet's life, such as, gestation, lactation, growth, maintenance or the words "All Life Stages.")

   (b)   *Animal feeding tests* using AAFCO procedures substantiate that (Name of Product) provides complete and balanced nutrition for ____. (Blank is to be completed by using the stage of the pet's life, such as, gestation, lactation, growth, maintenance or the words "All Life Stages.")

Understanding Pet Food Labels

(2) A nutrition or dietary claim for purposes other than those listed in regulations PF2(l) and (m) if the claim is scientifically substantiated.

(3) The statement: "this product is intended for intermittent or supplemental feeding only." If a product does not meet either the requirements of regulations PF2(l) and (m) or any other special nutritional or dietary need and so is suitable only for limited or intermittent supplementary feeding.

(4) The statement: "Use only as directed by your veterinarian," if it is a pet food product intended for use by, or under the supervision or direction of a veterinarian and shall make a statement in accordance with subparagraphs (o)(l) or (o)(3).

Consumers should purchase a food that is intended for the particular life-stage of their pet. If you are feeding a puppy or kitten, make sure the food is intended for "growth" or "all life stages." If your cat or dog is an adult, an "adult maintenance" formula or "all life stages" formula is appropriate.

Although products are labeled "Senior," no testing is currently required, nor has any senior profile been established. Senior foods conform to the Adult Maintenance profile.

Nutritional Profiles

Contained within the *AAFCO Official Publication* are Nutrient Profiles which are a component of Model Feed Law and Regulations. Detailed Nutrient Profiles are found for dog and cat foods.

Specific minimums have been established for more than 40 nutrients deemed essential in a canine or feline diet including: proteins, fat, vitamins, and minerals. Data is expressed either as a percentage or a weight measure.

For cats and dogs, there are different profiles for growth, reproduction and lactation, and adult maintenance diets.

Nutrient profiles apply only to foods that use "is formulated" in their nutritional adequacy statement.

Understanding Pet Food Labels

Pet foods are formulated to meet the specific nutritional requirements as set forth in the Model Feed Law. The Model Feed Law is presented as a recommendation to the various states. However, it is still up to each state to specify and regulate its own labeling requirements.

Nutritional profiles are expressed in two ways; on a dry matter basis and a caloric density basis. These approaches are used by companion animal nutritionists, veterinary professionals, pet food manufacturers, and persons knowledgeable about pet nutrition to formulate and recommend pet food diets.

Comparing Pet Food Nutritional Profiles Is NOT For Everybody

When comparing pet food nutritional values, it is best to use either dry matter or caloric density comparisons. This does however, require advanced knowledge of pet nutrition. These methods involve using standardized formulas and calculating and evaluating the results.

Most manufacturers provide nutritional profiles on an "As Is," "As Fed," or "Dry Matter" basis. Few manufacturers provide caloric or nutrient density values. You can calculate caloric density using the other nutrient profiles.

Dry Matter values compare foods on an equalized basis by removing moisture content from the calculations. (See page 25.)

Caloric density compares nutrient values based on a computed relationship to the amount of Metabolizable Energy in the food. Many pet professionals prefer to use this method of comparison because it compares energy and is independent of moisture content.

Summary

Pet food label content is regulated by the various state governments. Many states follow the model regulations in the *AAFCO Official Publication*. There are specific regulations governing nutritional content, words, claims, ingredient content, and presentation of information on a pet food package.

Understanding Pet Food Labels

As a consumer you will be able to make informed decisions based on the pet food label contents *and* the additional information available from the manufacturer. To find out more about product specific nutrient profiles, contact the pet food manufacturer.

For more information about nutritional comparisons on cat and dog foods, or basic canine and feline nutritional information, please contact PigDog™ Press at the address on the inside rear cover.

All AAFCO references are from the 1995 AAFCO Official Publication. To obtain a copy of the current publication send $25.00 to:

Charles P. Frank,
AAFCO Treasurer,
Georgia Department of Agriculture,
Plant Food, Feed and Grain Division,
Capitol Square, Atlanta, GA 30334

This section on *Understanding Pet Food Labels* contributed by Howard D. Coffman, author, *The Cat Food Reference*, and *The Dry Dog Food Reference*.

Pet Food
Math
Explained

Pet Food Math Explained

Introduction

This section is intended for the knowledgeable pet owner or pet professional who has the interest and knowledge to make use of the resulting calculations.

For additional information you are encouraged to refer to the *AAFCO Official Publication* or a textbook on pet nutrition. (See bibliography page 39.)

Dry Matter

All pet food must contain a certain amount of moisture or water for processing. In dry pet food, this is about 10%, in canned food, about 78%, and soft-moist foods, somewhere in between. Because proteins and fats, and other ingredients are given on the labels as percentages, it is impossible to compare pet food nutrients unless moisture content is removed. Dry matter comparisons equalize the nutrient values and permit direct comparison between differing products (by excluding moisture content). The result is suitable for an "apples to apples" comparison.

The dry matter comparison is especially useful when comparing a dry food and a canned food. An example is explained below and further demonstrated in the worksheet on page 47.

Dry Matter is calculated by taking the percentage of the nutrient and compensating for the moisture content from the "Guaranteed," "As Is," or "As Fed" Analyses. For example, a food with a "guaranteed" protein value of 19% has a moisture content of 10%. This means that there is 90% dry matter in the food. (100% total - 10% moisture = 90% dry matter.) To compute the dry matter equivalent of protein, divide 19% by 90% or the amount of dry matter. 19/90 = 21.11 = 21.11% protein on a dry matter basis.

Calculating Carbohydrate Content

For use with the Guaranteed Label, As Is or As Fed Analyses: Add percentages of protein, fat, fiber, ash, and moisture. Subtract from 100. Result is carbohydrate percentage calculated by difference.

Pet Food Math Explained

Please note that when ash values are not present, the resulting carbohydrate value is not reliably represented.

For use in the Dry Matter Analysis: Use the "as fed" value as calculated above. Divide this figure by the percent of dry matter.

Metabolizable Energy

Metabolizable Energy (ME) is the amount of energy available to the cat or dog after elimination waste (feces and urine) have been accounted for.

All to often, pet food labels and pet food brochures do not contain ME or food energy values. If present, you will likely see them expressed as kcal/cup (8 ounce cup) for dry foods and kcal/can for canned foods. Finding or determining kcals/g (grams) values makes for the easiest comparison between all types of packaging.

ME is expressed in kilocalories (kcal) and represents the amount of energy in a food. To calculate the ME of nutrients, use dry matter values.

If the goal is to calculate the ME for a particular food to know how much to feed an individual animal, the "as fed" or "guaranteed analysis" figures should be used for the calculations. This will reveal how many calories are in a g, kg, lb, or cup *of that food.*

The following examples use dry matter values.

Metabolizable Energy is calculated by taking the percentage of protein, fat, and carbohydrates and multiplying that percentage by known constants resulting in kcal/gram (g).

For protein, fat, and carbohydrates use the constants, 3.5, 8.5 and 3.5 kcal/g respectively. Sum the resulting kcal/g values; multiply by 1000 to get kcal/kilogram (kg), or multiply by 454 g/lb. to get kcal/pound (lb). These constants are specified in the *1994 AAFCO Official Publication* (p. 114).

Pet Food Math Explained

An example is explained below and further demonstrated in the accompanying worksheets on pages 49 and 51.

Math Refresher

$xy\% = xy/100 = .xy/10 = .xy/1 = .xy$

If $xy = 19$:

$19\% = 19/100 = 1.9/10 = .19/1 = .19$

Calculating Metabolizable Energy kcal/g

$(P\% * 3.5) + (F\% * 8.5) + (Carb\% * 3.5) = ME$ kcal/g

Dry Matter Nutrient	Energy Conversion Value kcal/g	Computed ME Nutrient kcal/g
Protein (30%)		
.30	* 3.5	= 1.050
Fat (18.89%)		
.1889	* 8.5	= 1.606
Carbohydrate (34.52%)		
.3452	* 3.5	= 1.208

Metabolizable Energy kcal/g = 3.864

Calculating Metabolizable Energy kcal/kg

ME kcal/g * 1000 = ME kcal/kg
3.864 * 1000 = 3,864.00 kcal/kg

Calculating Metabolizable Energy kcal/lb

ME kcal/g * 454 g/lb = kcal/lb
3.864 * 454 = 1,754.26 kcal/lb

Calculating Metabolizable Energy kcal/cup

To calculate energy values per cup, three pieces of information must be available: Number ounces in a pound (16), Food Density (oz/cup) and Metabolizable Energy (kcal/lb). Food Density is the amount of dry food in an eight ounce cup.

$$\frac{ME \; kcal/lb * Density \; (oz/cup)}{16 \; (oz/lb)} = ME \; kcal/cup$$

Metabolizable Energy kcal/lb = 1,754.26
Food Density (oz/cup) = 3.5

$$\frac{1,754.26 * 3.5}{16} = 383.74 \; ME \; kcal/cup$$

Pet Food Math Explained

Please note that Metabolizable Energy values can be determined via controlled feeding studies *or* laboratory analysis. Contact the manufacturer to find out how the ME was determined.

In any case, Metabolizable Energy that has been computed or measured will be within 15% of each other.

Caloric or Nutrient Density

Caloric Density also compares foods without moisture content. Comparison can be made between foods of differing weights or volumes and of differing caloric content. The data relates directly to the amount of nutrient in a specific amount of food that provides 1000 kcal Metabolizable Energy. It provides an indication of the amount of a nutrient available in a standardized amount of calories. It takes the energy density of the food into consideration.

Companion animal nutritionists consider Caloric or Nutrient Density the most accurate way to compare nutrients.

The amount of a given nutrient is calculated by dividing the nutrient content (expressed as dry matter value) by its Metabolizable Energy multiplied by a factor depending upon its expression as a percent or weight measure.

Calculating Caloric Density format from % (Proteins, Fats, & Carbohydrates) to grams

$$\frac{\text{Nutrient \%}}{\text{Energy Density (ME kcal/g)}} * 10 = \text{g}/1000 \text{ kcal}$$

$$\frac{30}{3.864 \text{ Kcal/g}} * 10 = 77.64 \text{ g}/1000 \text{ kcal}$$

Calculating Caloric Density format from International Units (IU), or milligrams & kilograms to milligrams

$$\frac{\text{Nutrient (IU or mg/kg)}}{\text{ME kcal/g}} = \text{nutrient}/1000 \text{ kcal}$$

$$\frac{18,069}{3.864} = 4,676 \text{ IU}/1000 \text{ kcal}$$

$$\frac{3.5}{3.864} * = .91 \text{ mg}/1000 \text{ kcal}$$

Pet Food Math Explained

Caloric Distribution as a % of ME

Caloric distribution is a relative figure comparing the energy producing nutrients carbohydrates, fats, and proteins. It may be calculated using the guaranteed analysis or the dry matter analysis figures and the percentages will be the same. The example uses the dry matter figures.

Calories are supplied only by protein, fat, and carbohydrates. Caloric Distribution provides a good indication of where the calories are sourced which can be a factor during different life-stages and situations.

The method described and demonstrated on the worksheets on pages 49 and 51 is the "Modified Atwater" method. Consult the AAFCO Official Publication for more details.

Be sure to use Dry Matter values as input to the following calculations.

To Compute Caloric Distributions as a % of ME

Take the nutrient Dry Matter % and multiply it by its Atwater Factor (Energy Conversion Value). Take the resulting number (nutrient kcal/g) and divide it by the Total ME kcal/g in the food. This result is the percentage of calories contributed by that particular nutrient It is known as the caloric distribution for that nutrient.

Protein Example:

$.30 * 3.5 = 1.050$

$$\frac{1.050}{3.864} = 27.17\%$$

Dry Matter Nutrient %	Energy Conversion Value (kcal/g)	ME kcal/g	Computed % Caloric Distribution as % of ME
Protein	.30 * 3.5	1.050	= 27.17
Fat	.1889 * 8.5	1.606	= 41.56
Carbo	.3452 * 3.5	1.208	= 31.27
		3.864	100%

Consult page 51 for a detailed example.

Pet Food Math Explained

Working With Grams

There are 1000 grams (g) in a kilogram (kg). To convert kilograms to grams multiply by 1000. To convert pounds to grams multiply by 454. There are 454 grams in a pound. One kilogram equals 2.2 pounds.

Calculating Dry Food Food Density to Ounces per Cup from Cups per Pound

For this conversion you need the Food Density expressed as cups per pound and the size of the feed bag. For example: Food Density (cups per pound) = 4.20 and the bag contains 20 pounds of food.

An example is explained below and use of the value is explained in the accompanying worksheet on page 49.

First compute cups per bag by multiplying the Food Density (cups per pound) by the size of the product package. Then compute ounces per bag by multiplying the size of the package by 16 (ounces per pound). Then divide ounces per bag by cups per pound to compute ounces per cup, expressed as the Food Density.

4.20 (cups per pound) * 20 (pounds per bag) = 84 (cups per bag)

20 (pounds) * 16 (ounces) = 320 (ounces per bag)

$$\frac{320 \text{ (ounces per bag)}}{84 \text{ cups/bag}} = 3.80 \text{ Food Density (ounces/cup)}$$

Converting Grams per Cup to Ounces per Cup

In most cases Food Density is expressed as ounces per cup. Sometimes as indicated above, it is expressed as cups per pound. There is yet a third method, grams per 8 ounce cup. To convert grams/cup to ounces/cup do the following:

$$\frac{\text{g/cup}}{454 \text{ g/lb}} * 16 \text{ oz./lb} = \text{oz./cup}$$

Example of 100g/cup:

$$\frac{100}{454} * 16 = \text{oz/cup}$$

$$.2202 * 16 = 3.52 \text{ oz/cup}$$

Glossary
Of
Technical Terms

Glossary of Technical Terms

Atwater Factors - Numbers that indicate the *metabolizable energy* yield of the three energy producing nutrients on a *dry matter* basis. Proteins are 3.5 kcal/g; carbohydrates, 3.5 kcal/g; and fats 8.5 kcal/g. This means that 1 gram of protein eaten should produce 3.5 kcal of energy.

Caloric Density - Cats eat to meet their energy needs. Pet food nutrients can best be compared to standards if the energy amount is kept constant. *Caloric density* values are based on units per 1000 kcal ME of the food. It's taking the amount of food that produces 1000 kcal ME and measuring the amount of each nutrient to a standard (nutrient profile) or another food. Pet food nutritionists prefer this method as opposed to *dry matter* because it allows *for energy density*.

Calorie - Heat required to raise 1 gram of water 1°Centigrade. A calorie is used to measure the amount of energy (heat) when food is oxidized. Because the *calorie* is so small, kilocalories (kcal) is generally used to describe food energy. 1 kcal = 1000 calories.

Digestible Energy - As food is digested in an animal, a certain amount of food is passed in the feces as indigestible. If the energy in the feces is measured and subtracted from the *gross energy* of the food eaten in a 24 hour period, the result is digestible energy.

Dry Matter - All animal food has a certain amount of moisture in it. To compare nutrients between foods, the nutrients should be converted to *dry matter*. This is easily done by subtracting the amount of moisture in percent (taken from the guaranteed analysis) from 100%. This figure can then be divided into the specific nutrient percent from the guaranteed analysis of nutrients to have a *dry matter* basis. Nutrient profiles are given in a *dry matter* basis - not "guaranteed" as found on the label. *Dry matter* profiles assume the food has a 3.5 kcal ME/g *energy density*. Foods much higher or lower than this need to be corrected.

Energy Density - This refers to the amount of kcal metabolizable energy in a gram of food (dry matter basis). This figure is

Glossary of Technical Terms

generally obtained through feed trials or by calculation using the *Atwater factors*.

Feline Urological Syndrome (FUS) - This describes a lower urinary tract problem that often affects cats. The causes and symptoms are variable from animal to animal but excess magnesium in the diet has been seen as a contributing factor in some cases. Part of the treatment usually involves dietary changes to lower this magnesium.

Food Density - This refers to how much a certain volume of food weighs. The value is usually expressed in ounces (avoir.) per cup or grams per cup. Using the *energy density* figures and the requirements for a particular animal, the number of cups or can portions to be fed to an individual cat can be calculated.

Gross Energy - When food ingredients are burned in a calorimeter a certain amount of kcals is produced. This is the *gross energy* of the food. The amount of kcals may vary greatly from what an animal can actually obtain from eating and digesting that food.

Guaranteed Analysis - Required statement on a pet food package that lists minimum protein, minimum fat, maximum fiber, and maximum moisture. Sometimes ash, magnesium, taurine, or other nutrients are listed at manufacturer discretion.

Ingredient List - List on pet food packaging that includes all the ingredients in decreasing order of amount. The ingredient in the highest amount by weight is listed first.

Low Calorie Food - A food with a low *energy density* that is balanced to an animal's nutrient requirements. The animal eats as much of this food as it would have another, but consumes fewer calories.

Metabolizable Energy (ME) - When food is digested, in addition to the amount of energy lost in the feces, a certain amount of energy is also lost in the urine and combustible gases. The *gross energy* of the food minus the energy lost in the feces, urine, and gases results in *metabolizable energy* or the amount of energy an animal

Glossary of Technical Terms

actually gets from the food for metabolism purposes. This can be measured for a food by keeping animals in metabolism cages and averaging the results or by calculating the energy using *Atwater factors* (which were determined using metabolism studies). The *ME* of a food gives more information about the food than *Gross Energy*.

Nutrient Profiles - List of the minimum amounts of the various nutrients needed by cats or dogs in their daily diet to maintain weight, health, and well-being. Nutrient profiles are listed in a *dry matter* format or a *caloric density* format. Amounts in actual pet foods can be more that listed to account for life-stage and activity, but cannot be less.

This applies only to foods that carry an "is formulated" nutritional adequacy statement. It does not apply to foods that carry a "feeding studies" nutritional adequacy statement.

Notes

Annotated
Bibliography Of
Feline Nutrition

Annotated Bibliography of Feline Nutrition

Key

BH   Breeders and handlers
PO   Pet Owners
VET Veterinarians, Veterinary
      Students
TEC Veterinary Technicians and
      other employees
NUT Pet Food Nutritionists

ALPO Pet Center, *Feline Nutrition and Feeding Management.* **Lehigh Valley: Alpo Pet Center, 1993.** Although published as a reference for veterinarians and veterinary students, this booklet is very readable and useful for breeders and knowledgeable pet owners. Although it is published by ALPO, the booklet makes every attempt to be generic. Graphs and charts are printed in color and are exceptionally well done and useful. Topics include basic principles, nutrient requirements, characteristics of commercial cat food, nutritional diseases, and reading the label.
(VET, TEC, BH, PO)

American Feed Control Officials, *Official Publication 1995.* **Atlanta: AAFCO, 1996. ISBN: 1-878341-06-5.** Contains state laws and Uniform Feed Bills as pertains to all animal feeds. Feed ingredient definitions, additives as well as current labeling laws are part of the publication. Minutes of the annual meeting and committee reports are included. This reference contains valuable information but it will not be easy for the typical pet owner, breeder, average veterinarian or technician to find the information and understand the significance of it. Pet food nutritionists and manufacturers will find this publication most useful. (NUT)

Bicks, Jane R. *The Revolution in Cat Nutrition,* **New York: Rawson Associates, 1986.** This book contains a <u>lot</u> of information on cat nutrition as well as on health and behavior. The material could be much better organized as the information tends be in bits and pieces throughout the book. The nutritional requirements are arranged by category then alphabetically for vitamins and minerals. The format is the same for each nutrient entry - what is it?, benefits, how much?, best sources, deficiency symptoms, and advice. Myths and feeding mistakes are also discussed. Some specific brands

Annotated Bibliography of Feline Nutrition

of cat food are mentioned. Of special note is a section on common cat food ingredients. Specific dietary idiosyncrasies of cat breeds are presented but many are just repeated feline generalities. There is a "fitness" section with homemade and dietary supplement suggestions of questionable value. (PO, BH, TEC)

Burger, I, ed. *The Waltham Book of Companion Animal Nutrition.* New York: Pergamon Press, 1993. ISBN: 0-08 040844-3. Contains chapters on dogs, cats, birds, horses, and fish with emphasis on dogs and cats. Excellent chapter on digestion and absorption although it may be too technical for a breeder or pet owner with no science background. People not used to reading scientific-type articles may have trouble with the format, the inclusion of in-text references, the reliance numbers and charts, and British spellings. (PO, BH, VET, TEC)

Burger, I. & Rivers, J. eds. *Nutrition of the Dog and Cat, Waltham Symposium 7.* New York: Cambridge University Press, 1989. ISBN: 0-521-33019-x. This reference is a series of research articles. It contains many statistics and complex graphs, and also in text references to other published information. Many articles have interesting and important information but the average person might get lost in the research format and jargon. (NUT, VET)

Case, L., Carey, D., & Hirakawa, D. *Canine and Feline Nutrition, A Resource for Companion Animal Professionals.* St. Louis: Mosby, 1995. ISBN: 0-8151-1536-9. Sections 1-5 are very suitable for anyone interested in pet nutrition. Section 6 is more appropriate for veterinarians and technicians or those with pets that might have a particular disorder listed. Glossary and Appendices contain much useful information. The book is published in two colors that makes reading easy. Each section contains appropriate charts and diagrams and key points are highlighted. Each section is referenced. Chapter 15 specifically deals with interpreting pet food labels that should be of interest to all readers. Section 5 deals with common misconceptions and fallacies where answers are documented.

Annotated Bibliography of Feline Nutrition

Unfortunately not all current myths were addressed - probably at no fault of the authors. Interest in pet nutrition and the aura surrounding it is unfortunately creating new "myths" daily! (PO, BH, VET, TEC, NUT)

Coffman, H.D. *The Cat Food Reference*. Nashua: PigDog™ Press, 1996. ISBN: 0-9645009-4-9. This is a comparative cat food reference with the pet owner in mind. It compares grocery, specialty, dry and canned foods. (Ingredients, Guaranteed Analysis, Dry Matter Comparison, Estimated Food Energy, and Feeding Guidelines of 347 cat foods.) Contains the "meat and potatoes" of the information as required by a cat owner or breeder. Also included is a section on Understanding Pet Food Labels as well as AAFCO Feed Term and Ingredient Definitions. (PO, BH, VET, TECH, NUT)

Lewis, L, Morris, Jr. M., & Hand, M. *Small Animal Clinical Nutrition*. Topeka: Mark Morris Associates, 1987. Written with the veterinary profession as the target audience, the first four chapters are of value to anyone interested in pet nutrition. These chapters cover general dog and cat nutrition in a way that a lay person would find informative; yet a person with more knowledge would find adequate detail in charts and graphs to add to their general knowledge. The Appendices contain homemade diets and human food nutrient values. The remainder of book (Chs. 5-13) deals primarily with dietary management of certain diseases and disease states with Hill's Prescription Diets. Individual chapters in this section might be of interest to a knowledgeable breeder or pet owner who has experienced a specific problem. (PO, BH, VET, TEC, NUT)

"Obesity in Cats and Dogs", *International Journal of Obesity and Related Metabolic Disorders*, Vol. 18, Supplement 1, June 1994. ISSN: 0307-0565. A series of research papers dealing with obesity in pets. Discusses practical management from a veterinarian's perspective. (VET, TEC, NUT)

Pitcairn, R., & Pitcairn, S. *Dr. Pitcairn's Complete Guide to Natural Health for Dogs and Cats*. Emmaus: Rodale Press, 1982. ISBN:

Annotated Bibliography of Feline Nutrition

0-87857-395-x. This book is a proponent for holistic or natural pet care. Several chapters deal with natural diets, homemade recipes, and special diets. Other chapters deal with general pet care. Contains "Recommended Reading" in the Appendix that contains references that promote the holistic approach. The appendix does not contain a bibliography that documents many "facts" presented in the book. This book should be of interest to anyone who wishes to "explore" the holistic approach to pet care or who has the time and inclination to prepare and feed a natural diet. It's advisable for the reader to consult with his/her veterinarian before attempting any specific treatments in this book. Updated 1996. (BH, PO, VET, TEC)*

Plechner, Alfred J., Zucker, Martin. *Pet Allergies, Remedies for an Epidemic.* **Inglewood: Dr. Goodpet Laboratories, 1986.** This is a first person account by a practicing veterinarian with a special interest in allergies in pets and most specifically food allergies. He discusses allergies as a series of "examples" from his own experience. (They are not detailed or documented enough to be called "case histories.") This book was written at the time when pet food companies were proliferating and were adding ingredients to "please" the consumer - some of which were unnecessary or actually unhealthy for pets. Much of the valid information in this book has now been scientifically researched and is accepted by the veterinary community.

For the book to be entirely credible to a knowledgeable reader, it should be redone with complete case histories and scientifically acceptable references. (While this book has some excellent information in it, there is too much misleading and undocumented information to make it useful.) (PO, BH, VET, TEC with reservations)

Pond, W.G., Church, D.C., Pond, K.R. *Basic Animal Nutrition and Feeding.* **New York: John Wiley & Sons, 1995.** An animal nutrition text written for animal science students. Majority of the text focuses on agricultural animals. It does have a considerable amount of chemistry in its chapters on the individual nutrients and energy.

Annotated Bibliography of Feline Nutrition

There is a chapter on dog & cat nutrition, but it is very limited. Section on Feedstuffs and Diet Formulation may be of interest for those who feed dry pet food because dry pet food processing evolved from agricultural animal feed processing. (VET, TEC, NUT)

Simpson, J.W., Anderson, R.S., & Markwell, P.J. *Clinical Nutrition of the Dog & Cat.* **Oxford:Blackwell Scientific Publications, 1993.** This is a book meant primarily for veterinarians or technicians as it deals mainly with nutritional diseases and dietary management of clinical diseases. It does include a short and easily understood chapter on the anatomy and physiology of the digestive tract and also a chapter on nutrient requirements. The book contains technical material but it is presented in a way that is understood by an interested pet owner. Contains a good glossary that should help the reader. (VET, TEC, BH, PO)

Stein, D. *Natural Healing for Dogs and Cats*, **Freedom: The Crossing Press, 1993. ISBN 0-89594-614-9.** This reference with the holistic/homeopathic philosophy has a section on nutrition and vitamins and minerals. Included are home-made recipes. Each section is referenced but it is interesting to note that the references are mostly from other holistic practitioners. R. Pitcairn is frequently cited. For those wishing to look into this approach, this is an up-to-date reference. (PO, VET, TEC)*

Stein, D. *Natural Remedy Book for Dogs and Cats*, **Freedom: The Crossing Press, 1994. 0-89594-686-6.** Another holistic/homeopathic reference with somewhat more depth than the other book by the same author. Has a section on nutrition with essentially the same information as the previous book. (PO, VET, TEC)*

Waltham Symposium Proceedings No. 26., *Practical Nutrition.* **Leicestershire: Waltham Center for Pet Nutrition, 1993.** Proceedings from a Nutrition Symposium held 4/2/92. This is a series of research papers geared primarily for veterinarians or nutritionists. (VET, NUT)

Annotated Bibliography of Feline Nutrition

"Waltham International Symposium on the Nutrition of Small Companion Animals, Proceedings, Sept. 4-8, 1990," *Journal of Nutrition*, Vol 121, No. 11S, 1991. ISSN: 0022-3166. This is a series of research papers presented at a Nutrition Symposium. Some papers on clinical nutrition should be of interest to practicing veterinarians. Most will be of interest to nutritionists.
(VET, NUT)

Wills, J., & Simpson, K, eds. *The Waltham Book of Clinical Nutrition of the Dog & Cat.* Tarrytown: Elsevier Science Ltd. (Pergamon), 1994. ISBN: 0-08-042294-2. This is a large book printed in two colors (charts and graphs are in red) with larger than normal typeface. As the title suggests, this is a "clinical" nutrition reference, primarily for veterinarians. Despite its large print, it is written in a research format with many in-text citations and copious references at the end of each chapter. It does contain a couple of chapters that may be of interest to breeders or knowledgeable pet owners.
(VET, TEC)

*Advisory

Individuals making a home-made diet for their pets MUST have a SUBSTANTIAL understanding of pet nutrition and dietary requirements.

They need to know the nutritional content and value of all their ingredients to ensure that they do not over or under supply any specific requirement.

Those considering using raw meat and eggs in a diet, should also be fully aware of the risk of diseases and parasites carried by raw meat that can affect their pet. Many of these diseases are zoonotic and can be transmitted to the person handling the meat or eggs. Also, some can be later transmitted by the pet (who acquired the disease from eating raw meat) to the owner. These concerns are not always addressed by the authors of homeopathic references.

PetMath™
Worksheets

PetMath™   Calculating Dry Matter Values

Dry Matter

comparisons provide a mathematical method to remove moisture content so that differing pet foods can be compared on an *equalized* basis.

This is one of the ways veterianarians and pet food nutritionists compare foods. It is more accurate and representative of the food content than either a "guaranteed," "as is," or "as fed" analysis.

Use the "guaranteed," "as is," or "as fed" values as input values for this worksheet.

Review page 25 for additional information.

STEP 1: Enter nutrient name in column ❶
STEP 2: Enter nutrient value in column ❷ in %
STEP 3: Enter food moisture content in column ❸ in %
STEP4: Calculate Dry Matter Content
Subtract column ❸ from 100% (100 - 10). Enter result in column ❹ (90) in %
STEP 5: Calculate Nutrient Dry Matter Content
Divide column ❷ by column ❹ (25 / 90) = .2778. Enter the value in column ❺
STEP 6: Express value in column ❺ as percent (.2778 *100) = 27.78%
Enter the result in column ❻
STEP 7: Repeat these steps for each nutrient you wish to compare dry matter values.

❶ Nutrient	❷ Nutrient Value	❸ Moisture Content	❹ Calculated Dry Matter %	❺ Calculated Nutrient Dry Matter	❻ Calculated Nutrient Dry Matter %
Protein (dry)	25%	10%	90%	0.2778	27.78%
Protein (can)	8%	78%	22%	0.3636	36.36%

PetMath™ Calculating Metabolizable Energy Values

Calculate Metabolizable Energy kcal/g

STEP 1: Enter Protein DM value in column ❶ as decimal
STEP 2: Multiply column 1 * column ❷
STEP 3: Enter Protein kcal/g in column ❸
STEP 4: Enter Fat DM value in column ❹
STEP 5: Multiply column 4 * column ❺
STEP 6: Enter Fat kcal/g in column ❻
STEP 7: Enter Carbo DM value in column ❼ (see p. 27)
STEP 8: Multiply column ❼ * column ❽
STEP 9: Enter Carbo kcal/g in column ❾
STEP 10: Add columns ❸, ❻, and ❾

Calculate Total Metabolizable Energy values

STEP 11: Enter Total kcal/g in column ❿
STEP 12: Multiply column ❿ *1000
STEP 13: Enter Total kcal /kg in column ⓫
STEP 14: Multiply column ❿ * 454
STEP 15: Enter Total kcal /lb in column ⓬

Calculate Metabolizable Energy kcal/cup

STEP 16: Enter Food Density in Ounces per Cup in column ⓭ (Consult Manufacturer or see p. 30.)
STEP 17: Divide ME kcal/lb by 16 (ounces) multiply result by Food Density. Place kcal/cup in column ⓮.

PROTEIN

❶ Dry Matter Nutrient Value	❷ Protein Conversion Factor	❸ Metabolizable Energy kcal/g
0.30	3.50	1.050
	3.50	

FAT

❹ Dry Matter Nutrient Value	❺ Fat Conversion Factor	❻ Metabolizable Energy kcal/g
0.19	8.50	1.606
	8.50	

CARBOHYDRATES

❼ Dry Matter Nutrient Value	❽ Carbo Conversion Factor	❾ Metabolizable Energy kcal/g
0.35	3.50	1.208
	3.50	

TOTAL METABOLIZABLE ENERGY

❿ Total ME kcal/g	⓫ Total ME kcal/kg	⓬ Total ME kcal/lb	⓭ Food Density Oz per Cup	⓮ Total ME kcal/cup
3.864	3,863.85	1,754.19	3.5	383.73

PetMath™ Calculating Caloric Distribution as a % of ME

USE THE METABOLIZABLE ENERGY VALUES CALCULATED ON (PAGE 49)

STEP 1: Copy Protein ME kcal/g from column ❸ (p. 49) to cell 1A
STEP 2: Copy Fat ME kcal/g from column ❻ (p. 49) to cell 2A
STEP 3: Copy Carbohydrate ME kcal/g from column ❾ (p. 49) to cell 3A
STEP 4: Copy Total ME kcal/g from column ❿ (p. 49) to cells 1B, 2B, and 3B

Calculate Caloric Distribution as a % of ME

STEP 5: Compute Protein Distribution; Divide cell 1A by 1B and enter result in cell 1C, express as %
STEP 6: Compute Fat Distribution; Divide cell 2A by 2B and enter result in cell 2C, express as %
STEP 7: Compute Carbohydrate Distribution; Divide cell 3A by 3B and enter result in cell 3C, express as %
STEP 8: Verify %; Add cells 1C, 2C, and 3C. Result should equal 100%.

EXAMPLE

PROTEIN

Protein Metabolizable Energy kcal/g	1A -->	1.050
Total Metabolizable Energy kcal/g	1B -->	3.864
Protein Distribution as % of ME (1A/1B)	1C -->	27.17%

FAT

Fat Metabolizable Energy kcal/g	2A -->	1.606
Total Metabolizable Energy kcal/g	2B -->	3.864
Fat Distribution as % of ME (2A/2B)	2C -->	41.56%

CARBOHYDRATES

Carbo Metabolizable Energy kcal/g	3A -->	1.208
Total Metabolizable Energy kcal/g	3B -->	3.864
Carbo Distribution as % of ME (3A/3B)	3C -->	31.26%

WORKSHEET

PROTEIN

Protein Metabolizable Energy kcal/g	A
Total Metabolizable Energy kcal/g	B
Protein Distribution as % of ME	(A/B)

FAT

Fat Metabolizable Energy kcal/g	A
Total Metabolizable Energy kcal/g	B
Fat Distribution as % of ME	(A/B)

CARBOHYDRATES

Carbo Metabolizable Energy kcal/g	A
Total Metabolizable Energy kcal/g	B
Carbo Distribution as % of ME	(A/B)

PetMath™ Dry Food Cost Comparison Worksheet

TO USE WORKSHEET FOLLOW EXAMPLE BELOW

STEP 1: Enter product name in column ①

STEP 2: Enter your local market price in column ②
$20.00

STEP 3: Lookup your product on the Worksheet
Reference Chart
Enter bag size in column ③ 20 and
Enter the Food Density in column ⑤ 3.5

STEP 4: Calculate Ounces Per Bag
Multiply column ③ by 16 (Ounces Per Pound)
20 lbs* 16 (oz/lb) = 320 ounces in a bag
Enter result in column ④

STEP 5: Reference the Feeding Guidelines section
and look up the Cups Per Day for your
breed and size
Enter that number in column ⑧. 4

STEP 6: Calculate Number of 8 ounce Cups in bag.
Divide column ④ by column ⑤
320 (oz./cup) / 3.5 (ounces per cup) = 91.4 Cups / Bag
Enter the result in column ⑥

STEP 7: Calculate Cost Per Cup
Divide column ② by column ⑥
$20.00 (price) / 91.4 (cups per bag) = $0.22 Cost / Cup
Enter the result in column ⑦

STEP 8: Calculate the Food Cost Per Day
Multiply column ⑦ by column ⑧
$0.22 (cost per cup) * 4 (cups per day) = $0.88
Food Cost Per Day
Enter the result in column ⑨

STEP 9: Repeat these steps for each food you
wish to compare costs.

① Brand Name	② Market Price	③ Bag Size (Lbs.)	④ Ounces Per Bag	⑤ Food Density	⑥ No. 8oz Cups Per Bag	⑦ Cost Per Cup	⑧ Cups Per Day	⑨ Food Cost Per Day
DRY FOOD EXAMPLE	$20.00	20	320	3.5	91.4	$0.22	4	$0.88

DRY FOOD COST COMPARISON WORKSHEET   53

PetMath™ Canned & Semi-Moist Food Cost Comparison Worksheet

CANNED FOODS

STEP 1: Enter product name in column ①
STEP 2: Enter your local market price in column ② $0.33
STEP 3: Enter can size in column ③ 5.5
STEP 4: Reference the Feeding Guidelines and look up the Cans Per Day for your food considering the number of cans needed for your cat's weight.
STEP 5: Calculate the Food Cost Per Day Multiply column ② by column ④ Enter the result in column ⑤
STEP 6: Repeat these steps for each food you wish to compare.

① Brand Name	② Cost Per Can	③ Can Size (Ounces)	④ Cans Per Day	⑤ Food Cost Per Day
CAN EXAMPLE 1	$0.33	5.5	1	$0.33
CAN EXAMPLE 2	$0.45	3.0	1	$0.45
CAN EXAMPLE 3	$1.00	12.3	0.5	$0.50

SEMI-MOIST FOODS

STEP 1: Enter product name in column ①
STEP 2: Enter local market price in column ② $1.00
STEP 3: Enter number pouches in box in column ③ 3
STEP 4: Calculate cost per pouch. Divide column ② by column ③. Enter result in column ④ $0.33
STEP 5: Reference the Feeding Guidelines and look up the Pouches Per Day for your food considering the number of pouches needed for your cat's weight. Enter that number in column ⑤ 1
STEP 6: Calculate the Food Cost Per Day Multiply column ④ by column ⑤ Enter the result in column ⑥
STEP 7: Repeat these steps for each food you wish to compare.

① Brand Name	② Cost Per Box	③ Number Pouches Per Box	④ Cost Per Pouch	⑤ Pouches Per Day	⑥ Food Cost Per Day
MOIST EX 1	$1.00	3	$0.33	1	$0.33
MOIST EX 2	$1.50	3	$0.50	2	$1.00

Publications & Products From PigDog™ Press

PUBLICATIONS   PRICE

PDP01	The Pet Professional's Comparative Reference Guide to Premium Dry Dog Food (1995)	$72.00 *
PDP02	The Dry Dog Food Reference (1995)	$35.00 *
PDP03	Doc Z's Canine Nutrition Primer (1995)	$12.00 *
PDP04	The Cat Food Reference (1996)	$45.00 *
PDP05	Doc Z's Feline Nutrition Primer (1996)	$12.00 *
PDP06	PetMath™ Spreadsheet Templates for PC's (1996)	$28.00 *
PDP07	PetMath™ Spreadsheet Templates for Macintosh® (1996)	$28.00 *
PDP08	The Dry Dog Food Reference DATA SHEETS (1996)	$35.00 *

COMBINATIONS & SPECIAL OFFERS

PDP20	Dry Dog Reference & Doc Z's Canine Primer	$45.00 *
PDP21	Dog Ref & Primer + PetMath™ SS Templates (PC or Mac)	$70.00 *‡
PDP22	Dog Ref & Primer + Dry Dog DATA SHEETS + PetMath™ SS	$99.00 *‡
PDP23	Cat Food Reference & Doc Z's Feline Primer	$55.00 *
PDP24	Cat Ref & Primer + PetMath™ SS Templates (PC or Mac)	$80.00 *‡
PDP25	Dog Ref & Primer + Cat Ref & Primer + PetMath™ SS	$120.00 *‡
PDP26	The Dry Dog Reference & The Cat Food Reference	$75.00 *

T SHIRTS (100% cotton) (see pictures below)

PDP90	PigDog™ T-Shirt specify: SM, MED, LG, XL, XXL	$18.00 *
PDP91	Sleuth Dog™ T-Shirt specify: SM, MED, LG, XL, XXL	$18.00 *
PDP92	Sleuth Cat™ T-Shirt specify: SM, MED, LG, XL, XXL	$18.00 *

* Price includes shipping & handling for U.S.A. shipments only.
  International customers, please contact us for international shipping rates.

‡ Be sure to specify MAC or PC when ordering Spreadsheet Templates.

PigDog™

Sleuth Dog™

Sleuth Cat™

PigDog™ Press

427-3 Amherst Street, Suite 331   Tel: +1 603 880 8639   Fax: +1 603 880 0723
Nashua, N.H. 03063-1258 USA   Tel: +1 800 775 0712 ext. 6111   Fax: +1 800 831 3647

PigDog™, Sleuth Dog™, Sleuth Cat™, and PetMath™ are trademarks of PigDog™ Press, Nashua, NH 03063